"The heart issues that you describe are right on...All servants, even those who are leaders can benefit from preparing a heart to serve."

Dr. Rodney Swope
Rod & Staff Enterprises
www.rodnstaff.net

"We often need a goad to cause us to stop and take the time to reaffirm our commitment to Christ and service others as a outflow of that commitment. This book offers good biblical and comical anecdotes to cause us to pause in our journey, reflect and readjust our hearts."

Elder Monica Keenon
iSucseed, LLC
isucseed@hotmail.com

"WARNING: WHAT YOU ARE ABOUT TO READ MAY BE DANGEROUS TO YOUR SPIRTUAL AND POLITICAL HEALTH!"

Apostle Bennie Fluellen
Overflow Ministries Covenant Church
www.omccministries.com

Servant Leadership

The Heart That Serves

Holly Spence

Unless otherwise identified, all scripture quotations are taken
from the **King James Version** of the Holy Bible. Scripture
quotations marked NIV are taken from the **New International
Version** of the bible. Scripture quotations marked NKJV are
taken from the **New King James Version**. All Hebrew and
Greek references are taken from The New Strong's
Exhaustive Concordance of the bible

Monarch Publications, LLC books may be purchased in bulk
for educational, business, fundraising or sales promotional
use. For more information, please email
monarchpublicationsllc@yahoo.com

Spence, Holly 2008
Servant Leadership The Heart That Serves / By Holly Spence

ISBN 978-0-6151-9190-4

Front and back cover designed by Timothy Hawkins
Back cover photo by Taylor Made Memories, LLC

In Loving Memory of
My Granddaddy

John William Ray, Jr.
Thank you for being a Servant Leader and a
reflection of the Father in the earth.
Your legacy continues!

I want to bring a finely tuned awareness to the distasteful attitudes in church leaders toward serving. As a leader in the kingdom of God that weight and responsibility is even heavier, your influence as a leader shapes the lives of people.

We give those that we have rule over, permission by our example. So if our example is skewed and not in alignment with the Word of God, what type of fruit are we producing? The years of poor servant leadership have produced a bounty of ineffective, insecure and dominant title seekers.

Jesus was our ultimate example of a servant leader. His action of washing the disciple's feet and response to Peter's smug remark should serve as the foundational lesson to our development of leaders. Luke 22:24-27 only further supports that servant leadership is an important qualification. *Now there was also a dispute among them, as to which of them should be considered the greatest. 25 And He said to them, "The kings of the Gentiles exercise lordship over them, and those who exercise authority over them are called 'benefactors.' 26 But not so among you; on the contrary, he who is greatest among you, let him be as the younger, and he who governs as he who serves. 27 For who is greater, he who sits at the table, or he who serves? Is it not he who sits at the table? Yet I am among you as the One who serves.*

This book serves only as supplement to assist with bringing about awareness and an introspective look into our own personal motives and thoughts regarding serving and leadership.

It's important as leaders we have the proper perspective of serving and exemplify *Servant Leadership The Heart That Serves*.

Holly Spence

Table of Contents

About the Author

With a passion to know, learn and live God's Word. My wife has been anointed by God to deliver His Word to His people.

A native of Cincinnati, Ohio, Holly is a graduate from the School of Creative and Performing Arts in which she majored in Drama, Technical Theatre Management and Vocal Music. She attended the University of Cincinnati, majoring in Chemical Technology and currently serves as a Product Manager for a major Global Software Company.

At an early age she received a revelation from God about bringing together denominations from all over the US to seek God in worship and praise. Pregnant with a vision to minister to women in 1996: Designer's Original was birthed.

My wife has a true servant's heart; she is committed to covenant relationships and has a passion for God's Word. She is a covenant member of Overflow Ministries Covenant Church where she submits and serves under the Godly government of Apostle Bennie and Pastor Delores Fluellen. She's an anointed psalmist, entrepreneur, and businesswoman. She's the mother of 3 beautiful children Heather, Jehoshua and Joshijah-rapha. She's my best friend and covenant partner.

Vinnie C. Spence

Foreword

Throughout Old Testament scripture, there is a recurring theme that resounds. God Himself emphasized and Jesus Christ taught it in parables to show one's motivations and intentions. It is so important that it is the area that is changed thus signifying the new birth. The Heart....! Then there is Jesus Christ announcing that while He was born King, His divine nobility in no way was jeopardized through a particular act. It is so important that he has determined one's greatness by it. Serving....!

These two themes are certainly not the personifications of Our God and Our Lord in the Christian community today! But rather they are least attended to as we build our entire lives and ministries around the politics both in the Church and in the Kingdom. As leaders, we hypocritically preach and teach service as long as we are the ones being served. In our feeble attempts to justify our insecurities, we have even created biblical positions for those who will meet our every need, from carrying our bags and books, to making certain that we are treated as royalty, rarely having to lift a finger in an effort to prove how anointed we really are. People all over the Kingdom and within the walls of the church have been duped and deceived by their acts of service often rooted in selfish ambitions of becoming the next in line to be served. But finally there is a voice that speaks the sentiments of Our God and Our Lord.

The scriptures are replete with references to the heart. The Bible indicates that it was the condition of man's heart that moved God to rid the earth of evil through the great flood.

Genesis 6:5 (KJV)
5And God saw that the wickedness of man was great in the earth, and that every imagination of the thoughts of his heart was only evil continually.

Our actions are more than what we do; they are an indication of the condition of our hearts. But not only are they an indication of our hearts, but they are the revelations of our thoughts.

Proverbs 23:7 (KJV)
"For as he thinketh in his heart, so is he: Eat and drink, saith he to thee; but his heart is not with thee."
Our righteous and wise God weighs the hearts of men and women not to embarrass them but to reveal to us the desperation and deceitfulness of our own hearts.

Psalm 7:8-10 (Amplified Bible)
"The Lord judges the people; judge me, O Lord, and do me justice according to my righteousness [my rightness, justice, and right standing with You] and **according to the integrity that is in me**. Oh, let the wickedness of the wicked come to an end, but establish the [uncompromisingly] righteous [those upright and in harmony with You]; **for You, Who try the hearts and emotions and thinking powers**, are a righteous God. My defense and shield depend on God, Who **saves the upright in heart**."

It is then from our hearts that we serve. Therefore, we must constantly go through heart check-ups through the Word of God and by the trying of our actions to reveal the truth of falsehood of our motivations. Service to God, God's People, and the Local Church must be measured not by our actions alone but by the intentions and motivations of the heart! As a leader or one who desires to serve in leadership in the church, I pray that you would perform your very own heart check-up as you ask God to search you through and through. I am very pleased that a true daughter in the house has not only put to pen God's heart, but also what she lives within the fellowship, as a part of the Leadership Team, where the barometer of who she is as a leader is always tested not by her actions; but the condition of her heart which is made known through her attitudes and responses to the challenges of being a servant leader.

WARNING: WHAT YOU ARE ABOUT TO READ MAY BE DANGEROUS TO YOUR SPIRTUAL AND POLITICAL HEALTH!

Apostle Bennie Fluellen

Acknowledgements

In January 2004, while on the way to San Antonio, Texas I read a book by Markus Bishop, "Financial Planning God's Way." As I read, I prayed that God would give me "God ideas" and witty inventions to bring increase to my household and my local church.

At the last breath of my prayer God responded, "You haven't done anything with what I've already given you." Suddenly, I saw the face of one of my church elders, Prophetess Monica Keenon. I knew exactly what God was talking about as I heard her voice, "Write the book."

I sat there and began to rehearse the reasons why I couldn't write the book. I began with the age-old excuse of 'not having enough time', and finished it off with 'I don't like to write and I don't have a desire to do so.' But God in His infinite wisdom, addressed each excuse one-by-one–

1) Get out of time. I operate in eternity.
2) You spit out documentation for a multibillion dollar corporation, who has made hundred of thousands of dollars alone from what I put on the inside of you!
3) Your excuses have buried the desire.

Now, that was the "BIG" one. It shook me. Suddenly, the power of God immediately came over me, as I sat on that flight to San Antonio. Then, finally I heard, "The anointing will come with your obedience."

There are so many people to thank for this **major** endeavor. First, to Prophetess Monica Keenon (Cuz Cuz) for speaking life to this project, staying up many nights to edit and affectionately going back and forth about what words to use when. Mi hermana, Melissa Allen for your online editing and support. My FRIEND, Traci J. Gibson for editing and adding additional work to my plate. My brother, Pastor Michael

Rucker, for your consistent love, support for Vinnie, myself and our family and thanks for preaching as long as the earth remains there will be **SEED ......TIME...and HARVEST**. I thank God that our lives are intertwined for eternity. Knitted and Committed!

Taylor Made Memories, Mi hermana, my sissy, Juanita I. Johnson, you're one of a kind.

Timothy Hawkins, son you are absolutely awesome! Thanks for your getting everything done in10 minutes.

My spiritual parents and friends, Apostle Bennie and Pastor Delores Fluellen (Mom and Dad) thank you for your example, wisdom and years of serving. Know that your *serving* has not been in vain. This book is yet another harvest of your seed from your daughter.

To my grandfather, John W. Ray, Jr. to whom I dedicate this book, thank you for being an example of a Servant Leader. Your legacy lives!!

To my mother, Winona Strong, thank you for love and support even when you didn't know what in the world I was going to do next.

To my children, Heather, Jehoshua and Joshijah-rapha allow the servant in you be prominent as you lead in your areas of ministry. God's manifested glory in your life is the success you should strive for.

Finally to the one that God has joined me to, the one that causes the sun to shine in my life on a rainy day, the hinges on my door, the core of my apple, the cream in my coffee, the sugar in my tea, the hydraulics' of my heart, the father of my children and the caretaker of my love, my husband Vinnie C. Spence. Thank you for your unconditional support and words of encouragement. I bless the God inside of you. Godliness exudes in your life as a man, brother, friend and husband.

Warning—Disclaimer
The examples in this book are fictional and are not based on any person, church or corporation unless stated an example of the life experience of the author.

Every effort has been made to make this manual as complete and as accurate as possible. However, there *may be mistakes*, both typographical and in content.
The author nor publisher shall have neither liability nor responsibility to any person or entity with respect to any of or damage caused, or alleged to have been caused, directly or indirectly, by the information contained in this book.

Servanthood: Position, Title or Worship?

"O come let us worship and bow down:
let us kneel before the Lord our maker"
Psalms 96:6

<u>Webster's Definition of Servant</u> - *one that performs duties about the person or home of a master or personal employer.*

<u>Hebrew Definition of Servant</u> - *eded (5650) from the root word abad (5647), which means to work.*

<u>Greek Definition of Servant</u> - *doulos (1401) from the root word deho (1210) to bind or bond, translated as slave or servant.*
The most popular definition we are familiar with is the Greek definition diakonos (1249) –an attendant, a waiter teacher, pastor, deacon, minister or servant.

Often we may have the opinion that a certain level of achievement or status has been reached if we have someone wait on us. In many churches, some people are looking to be elders, pastors or bishops and think that the title of servanthood should be removed. This conventional opinion has created murals of egos on the canvas of our churches today.

In every position within the church there is some level of servitude that takes place. A bishop or pastor serves those entrusted into their care, through counseling, development or building of faith through the Word of God, etc. Elders and deacons are put in place to further assist the pastor to serve the people of God.

Regardless of the title, bishop, elder/pastor, deacon, steward/trustee, worship leader, grounds keeper, director of the usher board, head armor bearer, chief of the sound ministry or children's church coordinator, you are in a position of servanthood. Some of the greatest leaders in the bible are referred to as servants opposed to a title, for example Moses, Joshua, Elijah, Paul, Priscilla and many more.

So often we have a spiked temperature of desire for a certain title or position in the church. We think that having a title makes us great in the Kingdom of God, or it makes us look and feel important in the Body of Christ. Changing our hearts and minds by the Word of God will produce a natural fever-reducing antidote to this unbalanced desire. Position and title come along with responsibility, persecution, inconvenience, flexibility, selflessness, a submitted life and a glad heart. We want positions and a title in ministry, but are not willing to commit to the sacrifice that it requires. We falsely believe that a position and title gives an increased level of respect.

If you need a position and title to make you feel important there is an inadequacy in you that must be corrected. If you get a title and position when you are not healed, you then could produce additional damage to your personal psyche or the growth of those you have been entrusted to lead. Allowing a position to define you will result in further devastation to your psyche or emotions if you lose that position or title. When a reconstruction or a shift in leadership is determined by the set man or woman and that position is eliminated or you are replaced, if you have allowed the position to define who you are, then you will take the changes In a leadership position personally. You will think the demotion or change in position is a personal attack on you. You will think that your season is up. You will think that you can't serve without a title. You will think that you can't serve in another capacity. You will not consider where the greater need may be. You will want to blame leadership for causing you to fail and leave the church. But there is something in you that you have refused to deal with.

"Wounded, dominant, insecure and selfish leaders, produce wounded, dominant, insecure, fearful, powerless and selfish people".

Maybe you don't have the issue of a title or position defining who you are. You may think that having a position or a title puts you *"in the know"- but* it's not the position or title. Most people today use a computer. Your computer at work is accessed through a personal password that is connected to your position or title. In a covenant family church environment there is a spiritual father and/or mother that serve as Pastors or Set Leadership who have children (the covenant family members). The children's position in the family gives them direct access to the parents.

Your position or title at work gives you direct access to specific computer files. The files that you see are determined by your responsibilities. You can have the same position or title of another co-worker, you can both have access to the server, but what you see, how much you see and where you see it, is determined by your responsibilities.

Likewise, in a covenant church family environment we are all children with different responsibilities. What we see, how much we see, and where we see it will vary.

Genesis 24 tells the story of Abraham's servant, Eliezer. Eliezer made an oath regarding where he was supposed to find a wife for Isaac. The Bible says that Eliezer was the oldest servant who ruled over **all** that Abraham had. Abraham was a wealthy man and had several servants. Eliezer held the same position as the other servants, but it was his maturity that gave him the additional responsibilities. Abraham did not say that Eliezer was his ***favorite*** servant. Eliezer was the servant who held the earned responsibility to choose the bride. This is the same concept in a healthy local church with a covenant family environment. There are not favorite children, only children that have accepted different levels of responsibilities. So it's **not about favoritism**. There are leaders in the local church that have accepted more responsibility. ***Responsibility does not equal favoritism***. *"For everyone to whom much is given, from him much will be required; and to whom much has been committed, of him they will ask the more"* Luke 12:48b.

As leaders, self-discovery and evaluation of our motives is important not only for our personal growth, but for the growth and impact that we will have on those that we lead. It is important that we ask God to examine us, try our reins and our hearts Psalms 26:2.

Is servanthood worship?

Webster's definition of worship is - reverence offered a divine being or supernatural power; also: an act of expressing such reverence

Hebrew definition of worship is – shacha (7812) to bow down, crouch, fall down, humbly beseech

Greek definition of worship is- proskuneo (4352) to fawn or crouch, prostrate oneself in homage, to reverence, adore

Worship is not just the singing of our favorite praise and worship songs or the lifting of hands in a Sunday morning service. Worship is a lifestyle. Our treatment of our co-workers, strangers on the street, and our family members reflects a lifestyle of worship. Adhering to the policies and procedures in the workplace reflects a lifestyle of worship. Worship is when our lives epitomize Christ. Our life must reflect Christ in all that we do.

Our very existence is to worship. We were created to worship; we were created to worship the one true and living God. Worship to God is done through our tri-part being of mind, body and soul.

"I beseech you therefore brethren by the mercies of God, that you present your bodies a living sacrifice, holy acceptable to God, which is your reasonable service" Romans 12:1. Service in the Greek (lateria 2999) is translated worship. Making a decision to become a living sacrifice is our reasonable "worship" as a believer.

Our bodies are to be submitted daily to Christ just like our spiritual walk. Our spiritual walk should be consistent and constant with no holidays, vacation or personal days. Allowing our flesh to lead us is equivalent to taking sick days. When we operate outside the regularity of the Spirit we are allowing the sickness of our soul to overtake us.

When you are a worshipper your heart is to serve. Do you want to be a leader contributing to the vision of the house (your local church) and operating in excellence? Do you want to increase or enhance the lives of those you are in relationship with? Then SERVE! You can't find a true worshipper that is not also a servant. You show me a worshipper, that same person will be the ultimate servant. Serving and worship are interchangeable and excellent foundational qualities in a leader.

Our daily efforts should work toward our daily goal, which is to please the Father. We please Him by operating in excellence on our jobs; we please Him when we help others; we please Him when we open our homes to others; we please Him when we love our husbands/children/family; we please Him when our finances can be used for the building of the kingdom and not being paid in late fees and return check fees; we please Him when we deliver the gospel; we please Him when we live the gospel. Our life *is* worship.

In Genesis 24, Eliezer bowed, worshipped and thanked the Lord. Eliezer had an understanding of serving leadership and worship that the modern day church doesn't teach. Abraham gave Eliezer the assignment to find his son, Isaac a wife. Eliezer understood that it was God that deserved his worship because it would be God that answered his prayer and it would be God that led him and empowered him through grace to fulfill his assignment.

Eliezer had great responsibilities within the house of Abraham. Abraham had wealth and so did his servants. Eliezer didn't walk around looking like a peasant of the town. In our homes our children reap the benefits of our success as well. Our children do not look like ragged paupers, but a reflection of the success and wealth that God has allowed us to receive. Eliezer had to reflect his master's wealth. If he did not, Abraham would not have sent Eliezer to his own country (representing him), to get a wife for Isaac, the beloved.

Eliezer's reflection of Abraham even extended into his worship. Genesis 24:12 states that Eliezer asked the God of his master, to give him success and show kindness to his master. Eliezer was able to recognize God's favor before he finished his prayer. Eliezer could have allowed his leadership status as the chief servant and ruler of all of his masters' wealth go to his head, yet Eliezer with all of his status didn't forget the God of his master. An example of Eliezer's library of experience with God can be reviewed in Genesis 22. Eliezer helped Abraham and Isaac prepare for a sacrifice to God, traveling up the mountain with him until Abraham said, *"wait here, the boy and I will go alone."* Eliezer knew that when Abraham went to God he always had a sacrifice; he had an unspotted lamb from the flock. Eliezer didn't see the sacrifice; the only sacrifice he saw was his only promised son. Eliezer remembered what his master's God had done for him and he was a witness that

God had done it again, so he bowed down and worshipped the Lord.

Just as Eliezer was dependant on and led by God's grace, we cannot do anything outside of God. It is His grace, God's divine influence on our lives to be what we have been called to be and to do what we have been called to do.

As leaders, we must ask God to turn our hearts back to Him. Ask God to show you, where you have allowed the need to have a title or a position greater, than the need to serve Him. God is true to His word as a redeemer. He will not turn away from you, if you ask with a pure heart.

❧ Chapter Introspection ❧

Prayer

Father God, give me a pure desire to serve you. Forgive me for allowing a position or title to be my focus and not the work at hand. Lord redeem me as a servant leader; cause me to become humble and not disillusioned by my flesh and the need for a title. Turn my heart back to you; turn it to the true meaning of worship. In Jesus' name, I pray. AMEN.

HEART CHECK

What areas within your heart need to change concerning servitude?

What has caused you to turn away from the true worship of servitude?

Journal matters of your heart.

BIBLICAL REMEDY & DISCOVERY

What have you discovered through reading this chapter, the Word of God, and in your prayer time with God?

List 3 practical ways you will put the above into action this week.

1.

2.

3.

The Mystery of Serving

"And whosever will be chief among you, let him be your servant"

Matthew 20:27

"But he that is greatest among you shall be your servant"
Matthew 23:11

The bible says that he that is greatest among you let *him* serve you. Isn't that amazing? This is one of the simplest instructions given in the Word of God. Do you want to be great? In order to be great you must serve. Author Bennett J. Sims refers to *servant leadership* as *"Velvet and Steel", a mystical blend of gentleness and strength. It is a paradox that gains by giving.*[1] God desires that we know all mysteries. Luke 8:10a reads, *"To you it has been given to know the mysteries of the kingdom of God..."*

Knowing all mysteries allows us to operate according to God's plan, within His intended purposes for our lives. In the gospels Jesus often spoke in parables, which were used as a vehicle to drive the "mysteries" in the memory of the people. The biblical truths of the parables were confusing only to those who weren't willing to accept the truth.

---

[1] Servanthood Leadership for the Third Millennium

Spiritual principals are repeatedly viewed as mystical and have been in debate for hundreds of years. This debate over the meaning has caused denominational division in the church today.

Webster gives several definitions to the word "mystery" **mys·tery** 'mis-t(&-)rE (noun)1) "a religious truth that one can know only by revelation and cannot fully understand," and 2)
"something not understood or beyond understanding."
I would like to rewrite Webster's definition with another. Understand that my re-write is not based on years of linguistic scrutiny of the English language, Latin origins, or early ancestral tongues, but based upon a very simplistic, practical meaning of the word mystery. *"Mystery" means mys' ry,* simply translated "Don't miss read."

Webster tells us that a mystery "cannot fully be understood." It would have been best for the definition to stop prior to that added suggestion. There are times that we cannot rationalize why something is the way it is, because our thinking is too small to comprehend. God's desire is for His "sons" to know. *"Henceforth I call you not* servants; for the servant knoweth not what his lord doeth…"John 15:15a.

We should pursue this knowledge of "sonship" like we pursue our educational degrees, financial stability and material gains. The bible says in Proverbs 4:7, "*Wisdom is the principal thing; therefore get wisdom. And in all your getting, get understanding.*" I thank God that His desire is not for His word to be an enigma, and misread by His children.

Serving is simply the heartbeat of God, "*…but by love serve one another*". Galatians 5:13b. Our servitude allows God legal access in the earth, through his servants, to tend to the gardens of His people. Service encompasses encouragement, counseling, love and discipline that gives the knowledge of how to cultivate and produce positive growth. Love and discipline helps till the earth. Keeping the garden through active service actually makes it easier for God to water our gardens by HIS Word.

The Apostle John: a leader personally groomed by Jesus, gives the account of Jesus washing the feet of his disciples before the last supper. This is the most mentioned and famous example of serving in the gospels. It was customary for a host to have their servant wash the feet of guests when they entered the home. This washing would rid the feet of the dust and elements picked up while walking on the dirt roads. Remember, there were no paved streets, black top highways or sidewalks. All the paths were dirt and people as well as animals traveled the roads. Without completely being graphic, the excrement of those animals and people would be on those dirt roads. Washing feet was considered to be the lowest task of a servant in the home. The fragrance of distain can be smelled while reading Peter's initial refusal of Jesus washing his feet. Jesus replied with *"If I do not wash you, you have no part with Me." John 13:8.*

Jesus' washing of the disciple's feet was an outward sign of the inner washing that Christ wants to do with our hearts. God's washing of our hearts and watering with His word allows us daily communion with him. *"Though many yearn to be part of God's purpose, they fail to understand that our involvement with God's purposes flows out of our intimacy with God"* [2]. With each washing the mysteries of

---

[2] For God's Sake Grow Up! A Call to Spiritual Maturity Author David Ravenhill

the kingdom are open and understanding of a true biblical servant, "eded" (5650) and "doulos" (1401) can be reveled.

The Greek word for servant Doulos (doo-loss) denotes one in bondage. However, this service was often voluntary, and a person would willingly offer to be subordinate and obedient to another. Is this a mystery? Or would we say just stupid? Why would you give up your will and be obedient to another? Oh how we sing, *"to be more like Him"*, oh how we sing, *"Lord I am available..."*, oh how we sing, *"Use me Lord".* But as leaders or layman, when it comes to the metamorphic process, of changing our hearts and transformation of our lives to accomplish this, we begin to complain, we come up with excuses, spiritually disguised as: "I am not called to this"! "This is just not my season", "My season is up in this area", or "I hear God calling me to greater works." (Servitude is our calling; we just need to know our measure. See the next chapter)

If you can't be faithful over a few things (serve) how can you be ruler over many (to be served)? It's not the title or the work of a servant that causes one to be in bondage, but its *ignorance that will keep you bound.*[3]

Sacrificial giving of ourselves to others reiterates the fact that our treasures are not stored up for earthly rewards. Denial of ourselves gives God the ultimate glory allowing His workmanship to shine through. This type of giving is what should be considered "the norm", one of the foundational principles that is injected into leadership classes.

As our revelatory understanding of servitude increases, the intimidation or humiliation of being associated as a servant will dissipate. This growth is synonymous with maturity. With this maturity we understand that we are not *"eded"* (a slave) but a "son". We can operate, as a servant with certitude and our willingness to serve in any capacity will also become our heart's desire.

When we have this mystery of servanthood under our belt, and have surpassed this stage of revelation, then we are ready for our territory to be enlarged. However, our

---

[3] Apostle Bennie Fluellen July 10, 2005 Overflow Ministries Covenant Church Cincinnati, Ohio

territory can not be enlarged unless we go through the fire. In a firing process hidden impurities are consumed so that the quality of the object can be revealed.

After the firing process the object must be stretched and expanded to the desired shape. If the desired shape is not gained prior to the object being cooled, it may require that the object be placed back in the fire for the process to be repeated.

So, if you're not willing to be stretched, blown, rolled, cut on and returned to the fire…don't ask God to enlarge your territory. You must complete the entire process in order to graduate to the next level.

If God has given you a great vision for a ministry, serve another man's vision. If God has given you an idea concerning a business venture, serve another and help establish his/her business. This is the basic principle of sowing and reaping. As long as the earth remains there will always be **SEED ……TIME…and HARVEST**.

Going through our fiery process while serving another can be a blessing, we can glean knowledge from the one we are serving, and potentially avoid pit falls. God also uses this time to try, test and build our character. What better place to do it then while cleaning the church, filing, or answering the church phone. It's easier to clean the church than it is to teach the Church. In teaching you have the souls of the people in your hands. If you can't be trusted to consistently do the simple things, why should you be given greater things? Wouldn't you prefer for God to groom, nurture, cut and prune you while cleaning the church instead of in front of the Church?

I have learned valuable lessons through God exposing my heart privately and not openly to see its deceptive and wicked ways. For the heart is deceitfully wicked who can know it.

We always want the prophetic words over our lives to tell us about how great we are or where God sees us in the future, but we don't want to endure the journey to get there. If you have ever received a prophetic word then you can bear witness to the fact that after receiving the word everything seems to go in reverse. You find yourself asking God; "How long?", "What about this?", "What about that?", "Daddy God, You said this," and "You said that."

These are the times that you have to hold on to the Word of God like no other.

Genesis 37 tells of the dream God gave to Joseph regarding his future. After sharing the dream with his brothers they were jealous of him even more. Joseph went through a time of persecution, imprisonment, and accusation. Joseph was on a roller coaster of persecution and elevation. He would be broken down and lifted up each time to a place of importance until he was finally lifted to his place of eminence as God had promised in his dream. Joseph served with excellence in every circumstance of spoken accusations and imprisonment. Joseph weathered the storm and his character was proven by fire. Joseph was faithful over a few things, so that he could be trusted with **ALL** that Egypt had. Joseph's territory was enlarged.

What we often view as mystery is not a mystery at all. It is just not typical or standard, as society dictates. We often follow societal norms in an effort not to stand out and to be just like everyone else. But, as a leader we are not like everyone else. We are to set the norms with our actions to be viewed as normal and acceptable and not the other way around. The world is corrupt, accepts anything, and wants to say it's all in the name of "love" (because God is love). We have been set apart: as peculiar people and a royal priesthood. Our standards and abandonment of ourselves should not be viewed as stupid or crazy, but enlightening and fulfilling. Our level of influence should be prominent at all times (this will be pleasing unto the Father, pleasing to our creator and pleasing unto the savior, our Lord Jesus Christ) to show the world that Jesus dying was not in vain, but stood as a model of true service to others….the world. The ultimate example of servitude has been lost because we have done exactly what Romans 12:2 instructs us not to do *"…Be not conformed to this world, but be ye transformed by the renewal of your mind."* Before we can ever operate in the revelatory discovery of servanthood we have to change our minds.

The bibles says in Colossians 3:23-25;
"And whatever you do, do it heartily, as to the Lord and not to men, knowing that from the Lord you will receive the reward of the inheritance; for you serve the Lord Christ. But he who does wrong will be repaid for what he has done, and there is no partiality."

In fulfilling this scripture, the church will jump-start the conversion of the minds for the next generation; servanthood is something you cannot see until it is not there.

Regardless of your denominational status or title, I urge you; I implore you and I appeal to you servant leaders. Do not allow this spiritual principle of servitude to be mildly celebrated or strongly opposed. Serve the people of God! Show the world that the Servant Leader is the way of Christ.

"Lord we acknowledge that our minds need to be changed. Give us the necessary wisdom and grace to change our minds, for we know that we can not change what we don't acknowledge."

❧ Chapter Introspection ❧

Prayer

Lord God, I desire understanding and revelatory knowledge of you. I acknowledge my mind needs to change as a servant. Give me the desired strength and grace to be stretched, blown and rolled to the desired servant you will have me to be. Prepare me as you see fit so that my borders are enlarged for your kingdom and your glory. In Jesus' name, I pray. AMEN.

HEART CHECK

What has caused you not to serve or "misread" the heart of God?

Where have you been inconsistent in serving God?

Journal matters of your heart.

BIBILICAL REMEDY & DISCOVERY

What have you discovered through reading this chapter, the Word of God, and in your prayer time with God?

List 3 practical ways you will put the above into action this week.

1.

2.

3.

Heart of a Servant

"The heart is deceitful above all things, and desperately wicked; who can know it?"

Jeremiah 17:9

When the beating of the heart begins, it pumps around the clock to move blood through the heart and the remaining parts of the body. In the average life time the heart beats 2 ½ billion times without resting. This is one of many organs that have been labeled as a "mystery" in the medical world.

The heart within our physical bodies develops from the time we are conceived. The heart grows at the rate of the human fist. In each stage of development the heart takes on different shapes. It's not until the "fourth" stage that the heart has separated into the "four" chambers. Four is the number of weakness; it represents the weakness of man's salvation. *"The heart is deceitfully wicked; who can know it?" (Jeremiah 17:9)*

The essence of the heart is the blood. The arteries carry the blood to the rest of the body to provide the nutrients required for survival. If our heart produces bad blood, the rest of your body will be infected.

If our heart is not right concerning serving, it will show up in the rest of our body, as well as the church body. Infection will manifest in our behavior, infection will be evident in our conversation, and infection will become apparent in our walk. Infection will contaminate "our" body and "The Body "(church body) with which we are connected. The illness of our heart could ultimately cause death to our personal life and corporate life. This is why the psalmist said, *"Search me, O God, and know my heart; try me, and know my thoughts: And see if there be any wicked way in me, and lead me in the way everlasting."* Psalms 139:23-24

If you are sincere about God searching your heart, this "introspection" will guarantee an improvement in your quality of life as a believer, as well as bring about a commencement to a higher level of spiritual maturity. Several years ago, our Apostle approached my husband and I about becoming Deacons in our local church, we agreed. During our development process I requested that God show me my heart. Apostle made the statement "that was a bold request on my part". My desire was to please God, and I knew that the heart needed to be searched for my own personal growth and prepare me to deal with the new level of challenges the Diaconate would bring.

I prayed; "God show me everything; even things I thought I had previously dealt with. Situations arose, after a few days and by my response versus my reaction, I knew I was growing. I jumped and praised God; I proclaimed **within** myself, "I must have a pure heart". I went a whole two weeks with no incident that gave indication that there were still issues regarding my heart. Well after two weeks, (just as I had asked) God began to answer my prayer and He started with those closest to me, first my husband and then other family members. Each time God was faithful to answer me when I called. I didn't respond outwardly or loose my temper, but the incidents drove me to secret tears. I would ask God, "Why am I responding this way? I thought I was over this…" God answered, "You asked me to show you, your heart".

I began to rejoice in the Lord, thanking Him for His faithfulness to me. Weeks and months passed of various incidents arising. I responded with a new level of spiritual maturity, just by God showing me my heart.

Then the workplace test came. I was working on a major project; I had developed a documentation table of contents within 24-hours and had received approval from the client, along with accolades from the same clients for developing a reference outline based on their business processes only after having a two hour conference call. I had a very aggressive timeline. I developed and delivered over a 200-page document within a week's time. I delivered the documentation and had only one week after review to make changes, additions and deletions per the customer's request. The client within the week made several changes to a particular 20 plus step procedure, only to have the steps as I originally documented. I made several attempts via email, as well as voicemail to get the changes the client desired to make my deadline. Finally, I was able to have dialogue with the customer; even with all the frustration I was feeling, never once did I allow it to show in the tone of my voice or emails when conversing with the client. I even thanked them for getting back with me to ensure I could meet their deadline. Oh! How they thanked me and told me they appreciated my hard work and gave me such honor for meeting their unreasonable timeline.

The next day the same clients that gave me lofty accolades, the same clients that showered me with words of gratitude for my efforts, called my project manager and reporting manager and stated that "…they were unable to work with me and I was not delivering to them what was needed for the project to be a success…". They topped that with a bigger, bold-faced lie and said, "I was down right rude".

Well, I was out done, to say the least; I was just an emotional mess. I could not believe what was happening. I went from a cascade of accolades, to being off the project. In my professional arena, to be requested, "not to return on a project" brings a professional stigma. The one thing that worked in "my favor" was that my reputation had preceded me, and my manager was aware of my work and disposition with previous clients and co-workers.

For two days I was dejected and I cried at home privately and to my husband asking why this was happening. My husband questioned me and I questioned myself, going over every detail of the client's conversations. There was nothing that I could recall that would cause them to say this. On the second day of my emotional whaling, I asked

God what the problem was, "What did I do?" "I wasn't rude", God answered, "No you weren't". "I wasn't short in my responses to them". God answered, "No you weren't". I told God that I didn't do or behave in the manner that the client said. God answered, "No you didn't. But you wanted to...**that's your heart**."

I went into undignified praise; God was once again, faithful to my prayer and allowed me to deal with my deficiency with limited outward exposure. If you allow God through the Holy Ghost to show you-YOU, He will be faithful to do so. It's a wonderful thing to be able to declare that you have and can be thankful for a pure heart. God is faithful to make sure His children reach their potential and become the sons and daughters He intended. *Being confident of this very thing, that He which hath began a good work in you will perform it until the day of Jesus Christ.* Philippians 1:6.

The scripture, *"Search me, O God, and know my heart; try me, and know my thoughts: And see if there be any wicked way in me, and lead me in the way everlasting."* Psalms 139:23-24 came alive for me. I made an earnest request of God to show me my heart, His word to *"search me*" came alive, and the revelatory excavation of the scripture is truly light unto my path.

The heart has four chambers and each chamber has valves and vessels that are responsible to keep the body alive. It is important to have our heart fully functioning to eliminate the probability of heart failure or other frailties within the body. Plain and simple, "the condition of our heart determines the operation of our body". Serving is a matter of the heart. Your heart will determine whether you are a self-serving leader or a servant leader.

A self-serving leader's heart is easily detectable based on[4]:

- Whether you spend your time self promoting
- Self-interest
- Spending your time protecting your status or position.
- Not willing to share their job responsibilities or mentor someone to take their place.

---

[4] The Servant leader by Ken Blachard and Phil Hodges

- Not willingly accepting or receiving feedback that will enhance their ability to lead those that have been assigned to them.

Self-serving leadership is self-promoting and always desires the praise of man for service rendered. Self-serving leaders think serving will masquerade the unsavory, despicable, and gauche quintessence of the heart. Allow this chapter to serve as a caveat that everything done in the dark shall come to light. *"For whoever exalts himself will be humbled, and whoever humbles himself will be exalted."* Matthew 23:12
"For where your treasure is, there will your heart be also." Luke 12:34

A servant exemplifies the following scripture *"Do nothing out of selfish ambition or vain conceit, but humility consider others better than yourselves."* Philippians 2:3 NIV.
Serving is the giving of your self and giving just as serving is a matter of the heart not the condition of your circumstance.

A servant leader is a worshipper; only a worshipper can worship in spirit and in truth. *"Serve the Lord with gladness; come before His presence with singing"* Psalms 100:2. The servant leader serves with gladness, not with murmuring and complaining or an unwilling heart. Do you know a servant leader *impersonator* like this? Is it you? Always complaining, nothing is ever right, or no one else can ever do anything right. You're upset if you are not the one in charge or making the decisions, you are upset if you are the one making the decisions and no one thanks you for the job your doing.

Does this sound familiar at all to you? If you make these comments or hear the comments being made, the question comes to mind "What's your motivation for serving?" This is a matter of the heart, your way of thinking. Your impetus for serving is invigorated by the "thank you" or stimulated by the applause of men. Your spirited rage of enthusiasm is fueled by the hopes of titled promotions and when this is not done, your energy to "help" is zapped and your facial expression of happiness is like an ebb tide. The bible says in Psalms 146:5, *"Happy is the man that finds God as his help..."* You honor God with your lips but your heart is far away. Your worship is in vain and your heart is spiritually diseased.

Our heart produces bad blood that travels to other parts of the body, and bad blood contaminates other blood. So with our bad blood and diseased heart we seek out others to agree with us, bringing forth confusion and dysfunction. Each spirit or dysfunction brings about other issues such as envy, insecurity and strife. We are producing as a leader, but we are reproducing ourselves, a servant leader imposter. *"...As a man thinketh so is he..."* changing our minds and the way we think will deter the strongholds of our hearts. Strongholds are houses constructed of thoughts; the way we think and our environment all contribute to the establishment of our house's foundation.

If you know anything about construction, engineering or building a home, you know that the most important part of the home is the foundation. If the foundation is not built correctly the home will fall. So for a stronghold to become a house, it has been built on a strong foundation. If you are familiar with demolition you know that it takes less time to demolish a house than it does to build it. Even after the house has been demolished the foundation remains. When pulling down strongholds (the house of thoughts) it is easy to destroy, but the foundation will remain and it's important to get to the root of the stronghold, the foundation of the stronghold to utterly be delivered.

All that we do whether it's preaching or empting the trashcan in the sanctuary; we must let God get the glory through us. Our desire to serve should be for the glory of God, not the pleasure of man. Serve out of glory, not to please, for pleasure is the basement of your flesh[5]. God receives the glory through your attitude, consistency and diligence. There's a popular idiom that says; "your attitude determines your altitude". Everything we do reflects an image of an affirmative or unconstructive picture. People everyday view our images. The image will exemplify acceptable worship or strange fire. *Genesis 4:1-5.*

To produce a healthy heart or restore the heart just as in the natural you must exercise it with the development of the Word of God, you must flush it with the watering of the Word and you must release unnecessary tension with the comfort of the Word of God.

[5] Prophetess Monica Keenon, Elder at Overflow Ministries Covenant Church Cincinnati, Ohio

Training your heart to comply with the Word ensures proper function and beating of the heart for service. *"Train a child up in the way that it should go and when he is old he will not depart". Proverbs 22:6.* The child won't depart because his heart and his mind have been conditioned with the things of God.

❦ Chapter Introspection ❧

Prayer

Daddy God, show me my heart. Even those things I think I have dealt with bring it before me again to ensure that there is no residue in the lining of my heart. Cleanse my heart that it doesn't pump infectious blood through my body incapacitating me for your service and contaminating my sisters and brothers in Christ. Expose me in your secret chamber that I may acknowledge where I have missed the mark and receive forgiveness. Father give me the courage to go to my Pastor(s) and ask for their forgiveness for not being in my place. Make me not ashamed for I trust in you. . In Jesus' name, I pray. AMEN.

HEART CHECK

What contaminated blood have you pumped? How has it affected you and your local church?

Are you a self-serving leader? List what qualifies you?

Journal matters of your heart.

BIBILICAL REMEDY & DISCOVERY

What have you discovered through reading this chapter, the Word of God, and in your prayer time with God?

List 3 practical ways you will put the above into action this week.

1.

2.

3.

Are You A Servant?

"Just as the Son of Man did not come to be served, but to serve, and to give His life a ransom for many"
                    Matthew 10:18NKJV

The love that God holds for man is so great that he wrapped Himself in flesh and came to the earth, to live and die as payment for our sins. It was Jesus who ultimately gave himself as the sacrificial offering in order that our relationship with God the Father would be restored. It was this sacrifice that pleased the Father; it was this selflessness that caused the Father to say, *"This is my beloved son in whom I am well pleased."* Isaiah 53:10 confirms this by saying *"Yet it pleased the Lord to bruise him; he hath put him to grief: when thou shalt make his soul an offering for sin, he shall see his seed, he shall prolong his days, and the pleasure of the Lord shall prosper in his hand."*

This superlative surrender of Jesus' will to please the Father sets the painted canvas as an example for the Believer.

"For whether is greater, he that sitteth at meat, or he that serveth? Is not he that sitteth at meat? But I am among you as he that serveth." Luke 22:27

"For I have given you an example, that ye should do as I have done to you." John 13:15

"But made himself of no reputation, and took upon him the form of servant, and was made in the likeness of men." Philippians 2:7

"For even hereunto were ye called: because Christ also suffered for us, leaving us an example, that ye should follow his steps." I Peter 2:21

So what's your answer to the question **"Are you a servant?"** The scriptures are clear concerning Christ being our example and how we are to follow in His steps. If we are to follow after Christ and mirror who He is, the answer is obvious. God wants us to be servants unto Him and to be available for His glory. Service is a minuscule price to pay for what Jesus has already deposited on our behalf.

"For, brethren, ye have been called unto liberty; only use not liberty for an occasion to the flesh, but by love serve one another."
Galatians 5:13

In the mind of most people the word "servant" is synonymous with slave, menial or bondsman. But, for we that have been "called to freedom" (Galatians 5:13-24), grasp the spiritual implication that God has intended for his servants. Anything outside of this realization turns our freedom into opportunities of the flesh.

Not having a changed mind or being conformed to this world causes our thoughts and ideas to be perverted. Perversion leads to deception and destruction.

There are countless examples in the Word concerning destruction when the desires of the flesh are appeased. Following the flesh, impure motives, and selfishness (naming only a few) encourages rejection of the character of Christ. These behaviors inspire destructiveness that ultimately enslaves us.

Serving as a believer should be routinely unchanging. There is no struggle in this area for those that realize; "I can't do what I want to, when I want to do it." As we discussed in the previous chapter, this is a matter of the heart. The heart pumps blood through the arteries. Serving is one artery that leads back to the heart; it's the selfishness, the lack of love and inconsideration we have for one another that causes our level of servanthood to be deplorable.

It's the all time battle of good and evil, love or selfishness. Neither of the two can reconcile with the other. We have to make a decision to deny ourselves and walk according to the path of Christ who has been the definitive example.

This can be accomplished through Christ. According to the scripture it's already done. Galatians 5:24 reads *"And those who are Christ's have crucified the flesh with its passions and desires."* Our acceptance and decision to follow Christ ensures that a successful, Spirit-filled, subservient attitude can be achieved.

This is not a walk in the park. Changing habits and mindsets takes time. It is a process. However, we have to acknowledge that a change is required and we must make the decision to change.

Changing your perspective regarding being a servant and serving is no different than in other struggles of the flesh. The flesh must be crucified daily. To assist with this process it requires changes. Some of the general changes are as follows:

- Our diet, feed on God's Word. Just as in the natural, neglecting the spiritual food (the Word of God) causes our spirit to be emaciated and we begin to eat on whatever is readily available, although it may not be healthy.
- Our environment, we have to be around people that are like-minded, people that have the same desires to please God and bring honor and glory to Him with their lives. *"Do not be deceived: "evil company corrupts good habits."* I Corinthians 15:33 NKJV.

The blueprint that Jesus has laid before us identifies the behavior of a son. A son is only made when he is willing to do the will of the father[6].

Yielding our supply contributes to consistency and efficiency in building the kingdom. Additionally, it prevents the same servant leaders from continually carrying the full responsibility of the vision of the ministry. *"From whom the*

---

[6] Apostle Bennie Fluellen September 7, 2001; Repent and Come Under Government

whole body fitly joined together and compacted by that which every joint supplieth, according to the effectual working in the measure of every part, maketh increase of the body unto the edifying of truth itself in love." Ephesians 4:16

If the above scriptures reinforce what you already know or serves as a new discovery, use this time to repent and recommit your life as a servant leader of the Lord. Ask God to show you daily how you can serve Him. I am a personal witness that God is faithful to answer when He is called upon from the miraculous to the practical. Seek the zeal of God to consume you for His glory. Also seek the counsel of your Apostle or Pastor for opportunities to serve in your local church.

🍂 Chapter Introspection 🍃

Prayer

Lord, It is my desire to do your will. I want to be great in the kingdom of God for your glory. I recognize in order to do that I must serve. Give me the zeal for serving your people. Give the courage to change, give me the wisdom to correct where I have error in teaching others or in my inability to serve as you desire. In Jesus' name, I pray. AMEN.

HEART CHECK

Do you consider yourself a servant?

What is your definition of a servant? Does your definition line up with the Word of God?

Journal matters of your heart.

BIBILICAL REMEDY & DISCOVERY

What have you discovered through reading this chapter, the Word of God, and in your prayer time with God?

List 3 practical ways you will put the above into action this week.

1.

2.

3.

Anointed to Serve

"But the anointing which ye have received of Him abideth in you, and ye need not that any teach you: but as the same anointing teacheth you of all things, and is truth, and is no lie, and even as it hath taught you, ye shall abide in Him"

I John 2:27

The word "anointing" has become the "buzz word" of the 20th century. The word "anointing" is often used if our emotional follicles have been stimulated by the melodic sounds of a vocalist or powerful orator who effortlessly uses and weaves strands of words together as if he or she is lexicographer of the English language. However, the fact of the matter is that there are several well-spoken orators and dynamic vocalists, choirs, and musicians alike that sing and/or play well, but have no anointing. *Anointing doesn't fall its formed in character.*[7] There is no indwelling of the truth, no habitation of Jesus the Christ, the Messiah, the Anointed or His Anointing (John 14:16, John 15:26). The Greek word for "anointing" is charisma. Charisma in the Greek means to smear with oil, consecrate, and set aside. Webster's Dictionary definition of charisma (what

---

[7] Apostle Bennie Fluellen February 20, 2005 Overflow Ministries Covenant Church Cincinnati, Ohio

appeals to people) is what tickles our emotional follicles, but the "anointing" (from the Greek root word chrio) is what allows us to know the truth and the ability to try the spirit by the spirit. *"But ye have an unction from the Holy One, and ye know all things". I have not written unto you because ye know not the truth, but because you know it, and that no lie is of the truth. Who is a liar but he that denieth that Jesus is the Christ? He is antichrist, that denieth the Father and the Son. Whosoever denieth the Son, the same hath not the Father: he that acknowledgeth the Son hath the Father also. Let that therefore abide in you, which ye have heard from the beginning. If that which ye have heard from the beginning shall remain in you, ye also shall continue in the Son and in the Father. And this is the promise that he hath promised us, even eternal life. These things have I written until you concerning them that seduce you. But the anointing which ye have received of Him abideth in you, and ye need not that any teach you: but as the same anointing teacheth you of all things, and is truth, and is no lie, and even as it hath taught you, ye shall abide in Him".* I John 2:20-27

The anointing is what gives us the discernment to identify with others that are **abiding** in our Lord and Savior Jesus Christ.

When we have been anointed or have the anointing to operate in a certain area the illumination of Christ rest upon us. There is an ease and effortlessness that comes when we are operating in our area of "anointing".

In knowing our parameter of anointing or measure of grace, it's important to know our physical limitations and to ensure that we do not take on more then we can complete in excellence. For those that work with pure hearts and are readily available for the work of the ministry, must also find balance. This balance will give us the ability to take care of our family as well as our personal being. Taking an active role in finding balance will prevent burnout and weariness in our well doing.

Some suggestions for practicing balance;

1. Consistently set aside time in prayer with God (this is in addition to your prayer time in the car riding "to and fro").

2. Designate time for reading and studying the Word of God. Reading and studying the Word builds faith, promotes spiritual growth and gives refreshing.
3. Spend at least 30 minutes of quite time a day with candles, which produces a soothing and relaxing atmosphere.

The above list is not conclusive, but gives a starting point in bringing balance in the natural; while maintaining our household, serving the people of God, our local church, pastors and church ministries.

Additionally, keeping balance through the Word of God provides a "heart check". It ensures a renewing of the anointing on a daily basis. Our motives can be daily examined. Completing daily "heart checks" will keep us from crossing boundaries. When we play a significant role in a ministry or one of authority we have the propensity to over step our boundaries. Now don't say AMEN too loud just because you're not in leadership within your church body, this doesn't mean that you can't cross boundaries. With that stated; take a look at II Kings 5. This is the story of Gehazi the servant of Elisha. Elisha had healed Na'am the captain of the King of Syria's army. Na'am was grateful to Elisha and wanted to reward him with gifts. Elisha refused to accept Na'am gifts (II Kings 5:16). By verse 20 it is written that Gehazi crossed his boundaries. Gahazi took upon himself to accept gifts that weren't offered to him. As I studied this passage I learned that Gehazi in Hebrew is a compound of two words, which means valley of a visionary.

Gehazi as a prophet in training lost sight of the vision. Gehazi was no longer operating in the "anointing" of his position. Gehazi allowed the covetousness of his heart to cross the boundaries of authority and run after Na'am to accept, that which didn't belong to him. Gehazi was operating in deception. *Deception is false permission to act*[8]. If Gehazi had completed daily "heart checks" the crossing of this boundary may not have occurred.

Gehazi abused the authority that had been given to him for financial gain. **Every decision we make has consequences and affects those around us**. Elisha had to be tasked to punish his once trusted servant and the result for Gehazi was that he and his descendants were punished for his disobedience. Our decision to complete

---

[8] Prophet Kevin Leal June 5, 2005 Overflow Ministries Covenant Church Cincinnati, Ohio

daily "heart checks" not only affects us but affects our seed. If our seed is affected, then our harvest will be affected; if our harvest is affected then our prosperity is affected.

As an anointed servant other people can become obstacles that contribute to our unfaithfulness and weariness. Those persons that have not made a conscious decision to give all of their life for the serving of the kingdom of God can influence our decisions. This may manifest in the following ways:

1. Someone who is always attempting to find fault in what you do.
2. Someone who is unwilling to work with you cooperatively or if they work with you it seems as if it is more of a chore on their part.
3. Those that exhibit rejection and resentment toward you.

When we are operating in our anointing the spirit of envy will be magnified. Jesus experienced the same envy see Matthew 27:17-18. *Jealousy wants what you have; envy* wants what you have and wants to see it destroyed[9]. The root of envy is bitterness. This manifestation can be seen in those persons that are bitter because they've chosen not to do what God is requiring from them. Often these people can be identified because the farther the heart is from the heavenly Father, the farther it is from the spiritual father and from the people of God and the house of God will not be a priority.

Remember, we wrestle not against flesh and blood but spiritual wickedness in high places and principalities (a structure of principles).

Does the enemy have a stronghold on you regarding serving? Are you harboring or have you harbored bitterness toward a faithful servant? Has your decision not to make the work of the Kingdom a priority manifested as rejection of a servant or resentment toward one of your brothers or sisters in Christ?

Again, I urge you; don't be condemned but thankful that God would use the media of written word to expose your

---

[9] Prophet Kevin Leal June 5, 2005 Overflow Ministries Covenant Church evening service

heart. Repent, change your mind, Ask God now to purge you and wash you afresh.

The wonderful thing about God is that no matter what state we find ourselves, He is always ready to forgive. God the Father accepts us where we are and is constantly willing to accept us as ready vessels for His use. God recognizes us after repentance as a vessel of oil that can be used to anoint others for His Glory. His Glory is manifested by our lives and serves as a powerful tool of conversion for the unbeliever and believer.

Understanding our anointing of operation and the authority we hold when used properly can bring about healing. Review once again II Kings 5. In this same chapter we see the servant of Na'am's wife. Because of her selflessness Na'am's servant was able to direct her master toward his healing. The New International Version reads: *"If only my master would see the prophet who is in Samaria! He would cure him of his leprosy".*

What's more fascinating in this scenario is that this servant was what we would now consider to be a prisoner of war. Regardless of her present circumstances or how she arrived to be the servant of another, she knew her God would heal her master. What maturity this took and what an outward manifestation of the love of God in this young girl that she would altruistically share with her captors the knowledge of healing for Na'am's body.

In our anointed place of servitude our influence will bring about healing to those we serve.

Do you see how critical it is for the servant leader within you to arise? Do you see the urgent need for you to be in your place and stay there? How many people could have been healed through the knowledge that's inside you? As a servant there is much more impact then the church has recognized. This power of servitude will produce an effect that the world needs.

❧ Chapter Introspection ☙

Prayer

Father God in the name of Jesus please forgive my selfish attitude. Change my mind regarding my priorities. Forgive me, if I have caused my brother or sister in Christ to stumble. Forgive me, if I have caused them to shift their standard because of my jealously or lack of commitment to you, your house and your kingdom. Father, forgive me for my resentment and rejection of my brothers and sisters. God, I pray that my actions have not caused any irrevocable actions or attitudes. God cleanse me and show me daily where my soul needs to line up with my spirit and Your Word in Jesus' name, Amen.

HEART CHECK

Where have you crossed boundaries as a leader?

Who have you rejected because you left your place of servitude?

Journal matters of your heart.

BIBILICAL REMEDY & DISCOVERY

What have you discovered through reading this chapter, the Word of God, and in your prayer time with God?

List 3 practical ways you will put the above into action this week.

1.

2.

3.

PSS...!- Puppet String Servants

The title of this chapter may have provided you a little chuckle on the inside, sparked your interest or it may have even caused you to give a resounding AMEN. It even may have caused you to talk to yourself stating, "I know that I am not a puppet string servant, no one is going pull me this way or that way for his or her own glory". If that was your first response, it's probably because somewhere in your life you have been abused, taken advantage of, or spiritually raped. So, you have made a decision that never again would you serve a man or women that would take advantage or abuse you. Never again would you take the time you voluntarily devoted when you could be doing something else. Well, this chapter may be for you after all.

Puppet string servants always serve with a hidden agenda and are not always easily identified. It may take some time for the true heart to be uncovered. Puppet string servants serve to be recognized. They are always looking for a continuous pat on the back. I am not talking against encouragement and recognition. We should always be grateful to those that serve along side of us; we should celebrate their good works, their commitment and faithfulness. As a servant leader we should make it a point to thank our co-laborers and acknowledge that their work is not in vain. Numerous studies have been conducted that have proven that people perform better when acknowledged. A pat on the back is good, but there must be equilibrium to everything.

Puppet string servants are always saying *PSS(t)*…look what I have done. Puppet string servants will serve only when convenient and it doesn't interfere with their plans. They prefer convenience and opportunities to shine.

Puppet string servants are also those that will only show up for an assignment when certain people are in involved. Ooh, don't look now, but trouble may be ahead. You know the ones that will show their face to clean the church, but when Pastor leaves, they leave too. They are the people that work consistently and then are absent for three or four months doing just enough to stay under the radar. You know the ones that only respond to certain leaders? If a Deacon asks for assistance they are busy, but the Elder asks they are free. If the Elder asks for them to do something they are busy, but if the Pastor asks them to do something they are free.

If you serve like this, then you are a Puppet String Servant. You serve with strings attached. If this doesn't describe you, keep reading.

A puppet string servant is asked to serve and helps out, all the while keeping score, to remind the Pastor and Elders of all that they have done for the church. A puppet string servant serves maintaining a tally to readily whip out a score sheet for other members in the body; so when they are in need or need to be served, they can remind someone of all that they have done.

Puppet string servants are controlled by their emotions. Emotions pull them here and there. They are sick in their emotions. They have an illness and God wants to show them this illness because He wants to heal them. Your healing will allow you to operate according to the Word of God.

Emotions are good but when your emotions have been damaged based on your environment, past experiences, or childhood hurts – you are not whole and your pain has enrolled in your emotional pageant that those around you have encountered.

If you choose to work alone, preventing anyone else from learning your responsibilities (thinking this protects your position or title) you are a puppet string servant.

Every puppet has a string of control. Your string may be how it benefits you, your string may be; it depends on who ask me, your string may be; "who" is going to be there. This puppet's motive(s) are of an impure heart and a desire not to please God but to please man. So, you wonder why you are not teaching? Why you are not preaching? Why you don't have more responsibility? Why you're not a Deacon? Why you're not an Elder? Why you're not a Pastor? What would you produce? You wouldn't invest in another servant because you would function under insecurity and wouldn't empower people to grow in fear of someone succeeding faster than you.

The mentee should always be greater then the mentor. The son should always be greater then the father. That's the ultimate legacy.

If you think that this behavior prevents the spiritual abuse and you still have some type of control, you are deceived, misled, misinformed, hoodwinked, and taken in. **<u>Because you have strings, you're easier to control</u>**. A marionette has strings tied to each leg and each arm. Depending upon the design of the marionette there could be a string on the head, back and the backside of the marionette. It takes a matter of time to know which strings to pull to make the marionette dance or perform according to one's own desires. The puppeteer can loosen or tighten the strings of the marionette at will.

If you are a puppet string servant you should thank God right now that He showed you who you were in a book and not in front of the people. Repent, change your mind and operate in brilliance. Operate in the consistency of excellence God desires.

Ask God to show you your heart, expose to you those things that are not of Him. Ask God to send His consuming fire to overtake you. Give your heart an overhaul. Our goal is to be more like Him. Ask God to change your heart, cut your strings from your flesh and tie them directly to Christ.

Chapter Introspection

Prayer

God here I am a "Puppet String Servant" ready for you to cut my strings. God expose the strings of my heart to me. Work with me to actively change the motives of my heart. Give me a purity that will please you. Dig the roots of bitterness, unforgiveness and the need to control from my garden and replace it with seeds of love, faith and trust. Give me the desire to eat your Word that will snap the strings of impurity to my heart. In Jesus' name I pray, AMEN.

HEART CHECK

What has happened in your life that has caused you to be a Puppet string servant?

List the person(s) that contributed to you being a PSS? Now forgive and release them.

Journal matters of your heart.

BIBILICAL REMEDY & DISCOVERY

What have you discovered through reading this chapter, the Word of God, and in your prayer time with God?

List 3 practical ways you will put the above into action this week.

1.

2.

3.

Serving and Success

"This book of the law shall not depart out of thy mouth; but thou shalt meditate therein day and night, that thou mayest observe to do according to all that is written therein: for then thou shalt make thy way prosperous, and then thou shalt have good success".
Joshua 1:8

Due to the negative connotation of servitude, serving is often not coupled with success. Serving should be associated with success, because serving is giving. When we give, we are operating in a biblical principle that requires a return. *"What so ever a man soweth that shall he also reap."*

In order for the above scripture not to appear invalid, we should first reevaluate what success is.

Webster defines "success" as favorable or desired outcome; and the attainment of wealth, favor or eminence.

Joshua 1:8 states *"This book of the law shall not depart out of thy mouth; but thou shalt meditate therein day and night, that thou mayest observe to do according to all that is written therein: for then thou shalt make thy way prosperous, and then thou shalt have good success".*

The Hebrew the word for success translates as sakal[10], (saw-kal) to be (caus. Make or act) circumspect and hence intelligent: consider, expert, instruct, prosper, prudent, skill, have good success, teach, understand, wisdom, wise, guide wittingly.

In chapter one of Joshua, God tells Joshua as His servant what his success will be. He instructs Joshua to obtain this success you must *"Only be thou strong and very courageous, that thou mayest observe to do according to all the law, which Moses my servant commanded thee: turn not from it to the right hand or to the left, that thou mayest prosper withersoever thou goest."* Joshua 1:7 God promises Joshua that He would be with him just as He was with his servant Moses. God not only gave Joshua the promise but God instructed Joshua on how to be a successful servant, just as Moses, his lord before him.

---

[10] The New Strong's Exhaustive Concordance of the bible 7919

The impurity of the soul and the corruption of the world have tainted the minds of God's people, we do not view prosperity or success as God.

In the churches today we have what some refer to as the "prosperity message". This message has become a topic of contest because most preachers go too far or don't teach balance. The message of wealth and prosperity has generated millions, if not a billion dollar industry. Having this wealth is meaningless if your character doesn't line up with the Word of God.

Yes, we have been purposed to have prosperity, we are a prosperous people, just as the Word of God declares. *"We are the head and not the tail, we are above and not beneath"*. Operating in our principles of sowing and reaping will produce that abundant harvest. But as our Apostle has often said *"Don't let your purpose take you where your character can't keep you"*[11].

This phrase should be adapted for all leaders and believers alike. Ensuring your character lines up with the

---

[11] Apostle Bennie Fluellen, Overflow Ministries Covenant Church Cincinnati, Ohio

Word of God reiterates the need to have – "daily heart checks".

What does it profit a man to gain the whole world and loose his own soul? What does it matter that you have more cars than you can drive at one time? What difference does it make that you receive an increase and promotion on your job catapulting you to a 6-figure income and your life, your marriage and your families' life consistently doesn't glorify God?

Does it matter that you have a PhD? Does it matter that you own real estate that has the potential to retire you early, but your level of serving through the giving of your life (time, money, mind, body, intellect and emotions) doesn't equate to the day's work of an ant? There is a series of calibrations our mind must experience in order to bring the priorities of our life into the proper perspective of serving God.

We should be successful God's way. Following the instructions of God emanates that obedience is better than sacrifice.

The bible says, *"Seek ye first the Kingdom of God and all His righteousness and these other things shall be added unto you"*. We have to walk in truth!! That's why it's important to know the Word of God for yourself, so you're not *"tossed to and fro with every wind of doctrine"*.

III John 2 reads *"Beloved, I wish above all things that thou mayest prosper and be in health, even as thy soul prospereth"*. Health in the Greek is translated uncorrupt doctrine, safe, sound.

The above scripture settles the fact that we are to live successfully and have true doctrine, even as our soul prospers. It's the true doctrine that will allow our souls to prosper. The true doctrine of Jesus Christ is what causes our souls to line up with our spirit. It's this doctrine, the Word of God that will cause our priorities to shift. The Word will renew our minds as it promises and define our lives as God has predetermined.

Read Deuteronomy 11:18-32 to study the promise of success to the children of Israel. God tells Joshua a condition of the success; *hide these words in your heart and soul, put them in writing so you can see them, teach*

*your children, speak of my words in your home when you
get up in the morning, when you are eating, and before
you go to sleep.* According to Deuteronomy 30:2 do this
with your heart and your soul.

It is important that our heart is being checked on a daily
basis and our soul lines up with our spirit. This will prevent
us from making decisions regarding our life out of a
corrupt, unsuccessful or poor health (doctrine).

In reviewing those servants that were mentioned in
previous chapters, Eliezer and the young maiden (Na'am's
servant) were very successful servants. Remember in the
Hebrew success means, intelligent, prudent, to understand
and wise. They operated according the measure or grace
that was on their life as a servant. In both instances their
master's household was increased. One through healing of
the body, the other through the blessing of a wife (Whoso
findeth a wife findeth a good thing…that's another book).
Success was brought to the home they were serving.

Can you imagine the impact we would have in our
individual houses of worship if everyone operated in the
grace as a servant? Can you imagine the impression that

the church of God would leave on the world if our souls were prosperous?

There are those that are doing great exploits for God with pure hearts. That number would increase immeasurably if we all functioned accordingly.

It would be a quantifiable ignominy if I continue to talk about serving and success and not bring up Joseph. Whether a bible scholar or regular attendee of children's church, I am sure you are aware of the story of Joseph. Joseph was destined for success. God showed Joseph his future as a young boy. God depicted for Joseph his success and wealth through a dream.

The importance of seeing ourselves as a success and with wealth is the qualifier for being. Unless we can see ourselves in our future, unless we can see ourselves successful that outcome will not come to pass. The sight I am referring to is our belief or spiritual sight – FAITH. We as believers walk by faith not by sight. We have to believe to see the success and wealth for our life and go towards that end.

Joseph after seeing his future, he shared with his brothers all that he saw in his dream. You may know the story well. Joseph's brothers were not very pleased with Joseph's tales from the night. Joseph's dream was more of a nightmare for his brothers. They already had to contend with the favor that their father showed Joseph and now they have to hear him boast of them bowing to him. That was too much for the brothers to handle.

We should declare wealth and success in and over our lives in grace and humility. Like Joseph we understand that everyone is not going to be excited about what God has shared regarding our life. Not even family. However, we should not allow this to be a barrier or a sedative to our divine promises. Joseph's journey to success is embroidered with ups and downs, and hellish occurrences that cannot go unmentioned. Joseph's pathway to success was that undesirable development called "process".

We often want the promises of God, but don't want the processes of God. The book of Proverbs states "Wisdom is the principle thing, but in all thy getting, get understanding". *Your wealth and success is locked up in "getting understanding".* I implore you to embrace your process. Seven represents the number of completion; process is a seven-letter word. Eight represents new beginnings. You cannot get to your new beginning with out completing "your process".

Everyone's process is different. Joseph was thrown into a pit, lied on, and imprisoned. However, he didn't allow the conditions of his process build a wall of bitterness obstructing his view of the promises of God for his life.

There is a practical realization that we must accept prior obtaining our success,

1. It's not about you.
2. It's not about you.
3. It's not about you.

Our wealth and success is not for us. We will enjoy and benefit from it but we are to serve others with it. Joseph's ability to serve his brothers and provide for their needs is an example of the power of wealth and success.

Our wealth and success is for the building of the kingdom through giving in our local assembly or national kingdom building. We build legacy with wealth when we teach someone else how to build. This is the order of God in the earth.

If Joseph had not gone through his process and embraced the practical realization that its not "about you", then where would his family be? Where would the nation of Israel and their children be if he hadn't operated according to God's promise? How many legacies would have been lost? How many children would not been born in the land due to famine? Obedience produces harvest. Joseph's harvest was on the other side of obedience. You can never have a harvest without obedience.

Joseph's coat was an outward sign of favor.
Joseph's pit represents a dry place with no internal sign of refreshing. Don't give up in your dry place. If Joseph had given up in his dry place he would have missed his success. Everything was striped from him. There was no sign of external favor, but the favor of God was still on him.

Joseph's encounters were not happenstance. *When a man's ways pleases the Lord it makes even his enemies to be at peace with him.*

Joseph's brothers didn't believe in his dream. However, there were those that were not of the faith sent to bless Joseph. Don't think that because of where you have been you have no value. What Joseph's brothers meant for evil God turned it into Joseph and his family's good. If Joseph didn't have value, he wouldn't have been sold.

God will use anyone to bless us, even our enemies. Our place of famine can be so dry that there is no dew in the morning. No signs of refreshing.

No matter what or how the winds of life blow, do not allow interruptions in your serving. Joseph could have allowed the incident with Potipher's wife to disrupt his process and cause him to curse God. He could have thrown his hands up and said this is not worth it. The self-talk could have over ruled what God had already predestined. One of the biggest threats to our success is the "enemy" the "in-a'me" or "my inner me" Self-sabotage can kill our own success through fear, doubt, unbelief and lack of trust.

Stages or keys to Joseph's success, Butler, Baker and a Pharaoh.

- A Butler opens doors, someone to announce your entrance, shows you in, to prepare your entrance into your destiny
- A Baker takes all the raw ingredients, things that on their own they make nothing, but together make something
- Pharaoh, the one to finance the dream

Once we reach a level of succession we should not stop. One of Myles Monroe's infamous quotes is *"the greatest defeat to progress is success"*. Don't stop progressing at each level of success, look for your butler, baker and pharaoh. A three-fold cord is not easily broken.

God is interested in our prosperity. His pleasure abounds when His servants prosper. *Let them shout for joy, and be glad, that favor my righteous cause: yea let them say continually, let the Lord be magnified, which hath pleasure in the prosperity of his servant.* Psalm 35:27. Knowing that God is pleased, imagine how much more His pleasure is heightened when we as "sons" prosper in every aspect of our lives.

What we have been afforded the opportunity to do or achieve is not for us, but that we give back. Give and it shall be given pressed down, shaken together and running over. This is your overflow! This is *"Serving and Success"*.

Welcome to the Overflow!!

❧ Chapter Introspection ❧

Prayer

Lord God, bring me into your way of prosperity. Show me what successes you have for my life. I want to live in the overflow. Father God, heighten my level of discernment to recognize my butler, baker and pharaoh. Lord continue to show me the favor that rest upon my life and to operate accordingly. Father as I mature in this area of serving you, allow your success to rest upon me in all that I do. In Jesus' name I pray, AMEN.

HEART CHECK

How has your perspective changed regarding success and serving?

How have you been a success while serving?

Journal matters of your heart.

BIBILICAL REMEDY & DISCOVERY

What have you discovered through reading this chapter, the Word of God, and in your prayer time with God?

List 3 practical ways you will put the above into action this week.

1.

2.

3.

Index

Media Contact:
Traci Gibson
Overflow Ministries Covenant Church
10870 Hamilton Avenue
Cincinnati, Ohio 45231

Additional copies of this book can be purchased from your local bookstore.

Or email
monarchpublicationsllc@yahoo.com
include the following information
Name
Address
Day Phone Number
Number of Books

Visit our website
http://www.geocities.com/monarchpublicationsllc/
monarchpublicationsllc.html

Blogs
http://www.geocities.com/monarchpublicationsllc/b
log.html

http://www.101christianspaces.com/monarchpubli
cationsllc

www.ingramcontent.com/pod-product-compliance
Lightning Source LLC
La Vergne TN
LVHW011407080426
835511LV00005B/420